Sports

Soccer

by Nick Rebman

FOCUS
READERS

www.focusreaders.com

Focus Readers is distributed by North Star Editions:
sales@northstareditions.com | 888-417-0195

Produced for Focus Readers by Red Line Editorial.

Photographs ©: FatCamera/iStockphoto, cover, 1, 15; Fotokostic/Shutterstock Images, 4; JLBarranco/iStockphoto, 7; Brian Eichhorn/Shutterstock Images, 9, 16 (top right); kali9/ iStockphoto, 11, 16 (top left); Taweesak Jaroensin/Shutterstock Images, 13; Volodymyr Kyrylyuk/Shutterstock Images, 16 (bottom left); Jorge Casais/Shutterstock Images, 16 (bottom right)

ISBN
978-1-63517-922-4 (hardcover)
978-1-64185-024-7 (paperback)
978-1-64185-226-5 (ebook pdf)
978-1-64185-125-1 (hosted ebook)

Library of Congress Control Number: 2018931988

Printed in the United States of America
Mankato, MN
May, 2018

About the Author

Nick Rebman enjoys reading, drawing, and traveling to places where he doesn't speak the language. He lives in Minnesota.

Table of Contents

Soccer

Soccer is fun.

Two teams play.

They play on a field.

Players do not need much.

They need a ball.

They need **shoes**.

They need a **net**.

net

ball

shoes

Safety

Players wear **pads**.

The pads keep legs safe.

How to Play

Players must **kick** the ball.

They cannot use

their hands.

A player kicks the ball.

The ball goes into the net.

The team scores a goal.

One team scores

more goals.

This team wins.

The players are happy.

Glossary

kick

pads

net

shoes

Index